Callum Takes Swimming Lessons

Marcia Stanley
Illustrated by Sue Ann Erickson

Dayton Publishing

©2022 Marcia Stanley
Illustrations ©2022 Sue Ann Erickson
All rights reserved.

No part of this book may be reproduced in any manner without permission from the publisher, except brief excerpts used in the context of a review.

Set in Tuff (Stone Type Foundry) and Minion Pro (Adobe Originals); cover set in KG Love Somebody (Kimberley Geswein Fonts).

Printed and bound on demand, to reduce waste in manufacture and delivery.

Dayton Publishing LLC
Solana Beach, CA 92075
858-775-3629
publisher@daytonpublishing.com
www.daytonpublishing.com

ISBN-978-1-7351716-2-3

With thanks to Ryan, my son and right-hand man;
to Callum and his grandma, Sue,
who inspired this book;
and to the hundreds of families who have given me the
privilege of teaching their children how to swim and how
to be safe in the water. It has always been a joy,
fun for me as well as them.
— M. S.

To my little swimmers, Anders and Calder.
— S. A. E.

A MESSAGE FOR PARENTS AND OTHER GROWN-UPS

Callum Takes Swimming Lessons tells the story of four-year-old Callum's introduction to swimming. His teacher, Miss Marcia, earns his trust and uses his natural curiosity and imagination to help him feel comfortable in the water as he learns to swim.

The book is full of helpful information. But it is not a manual for teaching children to swim, nor for "drown proofing" children, which isn't possible. At the back of the book are tips for parents and other grown-ups, about swimming-pool safety and helping children stay safe in the water.

— *Marcia Stanley*

Chapter 1
Wednesday Morning

It was a bright summer morning, and Callum was just waking up. Today was the first day of his first swimming lessons.

Callum wasn't sure what swimming lessons would be like. But he got out of bed and put on his dinosaur swimming trunks.

He had some oatmeal for breakfast. And soon he and Mom were ready to go — out the door and on their way.

When they got to the swimming pool, Mom took Callum's hand, and they walked toward a tall, friendly-looking woman at the pool's edge.

"Hello, Callum. I'm Miss Marcia," said the woman.

"Hello," said Callum. "I'm not jumping into that swimming pool!"

"Oh, sure — that's OK," said Miss Marcia. "What if we go over there and sit on those steps at the end of the pool?"

Callum thought that would be all right. "OK," he said.

"Now," said Miss Marcia once they were settled on the steps, "tell me about your preschool and some of your friends there."

"At preschool we learn about dinosaurs," said Callum. "And some of my friends are Emma and Jackson and Noah."

Miss Marcia pointed to six little animals sitting at the edge of the pool. "These are some of *my* friends," she said.

"Callum," Miss Marcia said, "I'd like you to meet Fred the Fish, Louie the Lobster, Oscar the Octopus, Teresa the Turtle, Charlotte the Shark, and Frances the Froggy. They are quite special — magical in fact..."

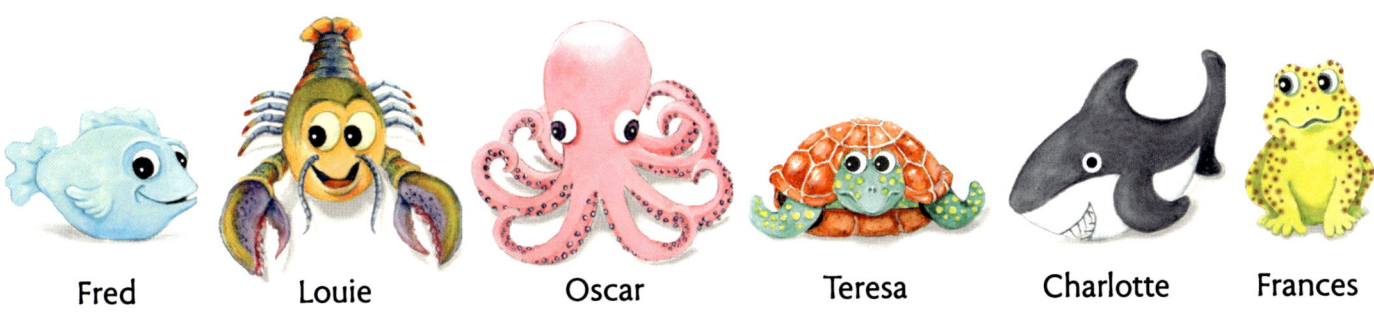

| Fred | Louie | Oscar | Teresa | Charlotte | Frances |

"Nice friends!" said Callum. He noticed a pair of blue goggles next to Fred the Fish.

Miss Marcia and Callum talked awhile. Then Miss Marcia said, "I'm going to pick you up now, OK?"

Callum nodded, and Miss Marcia gently and firmly lifted him up off the step.

"Let's take a look around this pool," Miss Marcia said. "I will always hold onto you. I will not let go of you."

As they moved away from the steps, Callum held on tight.

At the first stop on their tour of the pool, Miss Marcia showed Callum an underwater light fixture. "That's for lighting up the pool at night," Miss Marcia said.

After they had walked around in the water awhile, Callum was pretty sure he could trust Miss Marcia. So he loosened his grip a little.

At their next stop Miss Marcia pointed out a small opening in the side of the pool.

"Anybody home in this cave?" she called in a loud, deep voice.

"Anybody home?" called Callum.

It looked like no one was home, so they moved along.

"Our last stop is the Tickle Machine," said Miss Marcia. The warm water flowing into the pool tickled Callum's toes.

When they came back to the steps, Miss Marcia picked up Fred the Fish and held him close to her ear.

"Fred wants to know if you can blow bubbles in the water, Callum," she said.

And what do you think Callum did?

He had blown bubbles in the bathtub lots of times! He put his lips in the water, and he blew bubbles.

"Did you see Callum blow bubbles?!" Miss Marcia asked Fred the Fish.

Fred slowly shook his head back and forth. No, he hadn't seen it.

"Oh, well, Callum," Miss Marcia said, "I guess you'll have to do it again."

"Please pay attention this time, Fred!" said Callum.

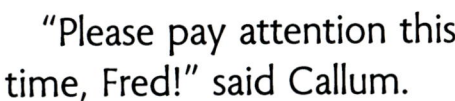

Callum blew bubbles again, and this time Fred paid attention. He whispered something in Miss Marcia's ear.

"Fred says he's happy you can blow bubbles, Callum," said Miss Marcia.

Callum was happy too, and proud of himself.

At the end of Callum's first swimming lesson, Miss Marcia told him two important rules:

1 When you're at the pool, **ALWAYS BE WITH A GROWN-UP. Never get into a swimming pool alone.**

2 **WALK — DON'T RUN** around the edge of the pool.

Then Callum and Miss Marcia got out of the pool.

Miss Marcia gave Mom a paper with pool safety rules for grown-ups.

"Thank you. I will read this carefully," Mom said.

On the way home from the swimming lesson, Callum told Mom, "I want to come back."

He was looking forward to seeing Miss Marcia and her friends again.

And he wondered about those blue goggles.

Chapter 2
Friday Morning

On Friday, Callum was happy to see Miss Marcia again. Fred the Fish and the other friends were there too — and the blue goggles and some colored rings.

"What are those goggles for?" Callum asked.

"These Magic Goggles are for you to use, Callum," Miss Marcia said. "They'll help you see better underwater."

Underwater?!

"Well… OK…" said Callum.

Miss Marcia helped Callum put on the blue goggles. She tightened the straps a bit, until the goggles fit snugly.

"Do they feel OK?" she asked.

"Yes!" he said. They felt fine.

"Now I'm going to show you how to put your face in the water," Miss Marcia said.

First she gently blew out her air. Then she breathed in gently — not a big gulp of air, just a normal breath. Then she held her breath as she put her whole face in the water.

"Now you try it with your Magic Goggles," Miss Marcia said.

And Callum did it!

Miss Marcia picked up Louie the Lobster and held him up to her ear.

"Yes, Louie!" she said. "Callum *did* put his face in the water. Would you like to see him do it again?"

Louie nodded his head up and down.

"Yes! Yes, he would!" Miss Marcia told Callum. "This time I'm going to count to five while your face is in the water."

So Miss Marcia counted as Callum did it again.

1...2...3...4...5...

They practiced this a few more times. Callum was happy and proud.

Chapter 3
More Learning, More Fun

After a few more lessons, Callum felt relaxed and confident in the pool.

Miss Marcia taught him how to float on the water. Soon he could let go of her hands and float by himself.

Miss Marcia taught Callum how to kick, so he could move forward in the water. Holding onto the kickboard helped him learn.

Next, Miss Marcia taught Callum how to relax and paddle calmly with his arms underwater.

Callum was beginning to swim!

Miss Marcia taught him how to lift his head up for a breath, then put his face in the water again and keep on swimming.

This took lots of practice!

Callum learned to jump into the pool, too. Miss Marcia asked if he would like to hold her hand as he jumped. He did, at first. But later he wanted to jump by himself.

Soon he could jump into the pool and swim across to the other side, taking as many breaths as he needed.

Miss Marcia taught Callum how to get back to the edge of the pool if he ever slipped or was accidentally bumped into the water: "Keep your **head down** as you **turn around** to face the edge of the pool," she said. "Next, put your **hand up** to grab the edge, and lift your **head up**."

Head down...
turn around...
hand up...
head up...
Safe!

Miss Marcia also taught Callum some safety skills he could use in deep water, to get from the middle of the pool back to the edge.

Sometimes Callum and Miss Marcia played games with the colored rings. Miss Marcia tossed the rings, and Callum swam down to get them.

Callum wanted to learn more. Miss Marcia taught him to turn over from a front float to a back float. And then he learned how to move his hands so he could swim on his back.

At the end of the last lesson of the summer, Callum told Miss Marcia, "Thank you for helping me learn to swim. And thank you to Fred the Fish and all your other friends — and the Magic Goggles!"

Callum climbed out of the pool and waved good-bye to Miss Marcia and her friends. "See you next summer," he said.

And he was pretty sure he saw Fred the Fish wink at him.

ABOUT THE STORY...

Callum Takes Swimming Lessons is about one child's first season of swimming lessons. Miss Marcia's goal was to take Callum from feeling a little wary and unsure, to the point where he felt comfortable in the water, able to get safely to the edge of the pool, and eager to learn more about about swimming.

By the end of this first set of lessons, he could float on his front and back, swim underwater, and lift his head to take a breath whenever he needed one. He had learned important safety rules and techniques for staying safe in the pool. And he had had a lot of fun.

The next summer, when it was time for Callum to take more swimming lessons, he was already confident in the pool. He was ready to learn other strokes, like the front crawl, back stroke, breast stroke, and butterfly.

Callum was ready to have even more fun in the water. And he brought his sister, Jemma — she was ready to jump right in and learn to swim too.

A FEW TIPS FOR GROWN-UPS…

Swimming can be great fun for kids, and it's also healthful exercise. But to help keep children safe, we need to understand some of the reasons things can go wrong:

- **Toddlers** are intensely **CURIOUS** and impulsive.

- **Young children** can get out of the house — **QUICKLY.** When young children get into trouble in the water, it's usually in backyard pools or spas, after they wander out of the house unnoticed.

- **Young children** don't fully understand the concept of **DANGER,** and can't be taught to avoid water. But as children get a little older and become aware of danger and of their own limitations, they can experience paralyzing **FEAR,** and even panic, near the water.

- **Adults, and children themselves,** often OVERESTIMATE a child's skill level. **Learning to swim does not make a child "drown-proof."**

POOL SAFETY

Here are some important things adults need to do to make pools safe for children:

- **ADULT SUPERVISION** is the most important safety responsibility. Make sure there is always **someone in charge of watching the children in the pool** — off the phone and paying attention to all of them.

- **NEVER LEAVE A CHILD** (of any age) **ALONE** in the pool or spa, even for "just a second." (And never leave a very young child — younger than 12 months — alone even in a wading pool or bathtub. Very young children can drown in just a few inches of water.)

- Make sure that you and any children at the pool **KNOW HOW DEEP** the water is in all parts of the pool. Point out "landmarks" they can use to remember where the water is deep and where it's shallow.

- Make sure children understand there is **NO DIVING** headfirst into shallow water.

- Remind kids about the **"WALK, DON'T RUN"** rule around the pool. And keep the pool area clear of toys and other objects so no one will trip and fall.

- Parents, babysitters, and pool guardians should **KNOW CPR**.
- Keep a **TELEPHONE** near the pool for emergencies. And teach even small children how to phone for help — how to **CALL 911**.
- **SECURE** all gates, doors, and windows leading to the pool area. And make sure they are self-latching above a child's reach.
- **KEEP** chairs and other things children can climb on **AWAY** from pool fences and gates.
- **REMOVE** all inflatables, beach balls, and other toys from the pool after each use. Otherwise, chidren may see a favorite toy in the water and go into the pool to get it.
- **DRAIN** standing water from pool safety covers.

ABOUT THE AUTHOR

Marcia Stanley started giving swimming lessons in her parents' backyard pool when she was in high school. Her reputation spread, and every summer the number of families taking lessons with Marcia grew.

Developed over the years, Marcia's approach to teaching children to swim combines a strong background in child development, firsthand knowledge of how children of various ages and personalities learn to swim, and years of experience giving lessons. Her teaching approach emphasizes developing trust and building on each child's interests, imagination, and innate curiosity. In addition to offering swimming lessons to all ages, she taught preschool for many years.

An experienced and patient instructor, Marcia lives in San Diego, California. She wrote this book because she feels strongly about the advantages of learning to swim. "While most people look at swimming as a recreational activity," she says, "it's also a safety measure. All children should learn how to swim."

ABOUT THE ILLUSTRATOR

Sue Ann Erickson is a graphic designer, illustrator, and fine artist. She is skilled in painting realistic watercolor images and in blending traditional media with digital illustration and design. *Callum Takes Swimming Lessons* is her fourth book with Dayton Publishing. The others are *Three Tales, Four Dogs*; *Playmates for Puppies, with a Family Guide to Dog Park Etiquette*; and *Grammy! Grammy! and the Magic Hat*.

The mother of four grown children and grandmother of two grandsons, she lives in Washington, New Jersey. You can see more of Sue Ann's illustrations and watercolors on Facebook.com and Instagram.com.

Made in the USA
Middletown, DE
14 March 2022

62649876R00022